FRIENDS OF ACPL

7-12-72

THE REAL CHRISTMAS

PAT BOONE

THE REAL CHRISTMAS

Fleming H. Revell Company
Old Tappan, New Jersey

Scripture references in this volume are from *The Living Bible* by Kenneth N. Taylor © copyright 1971, and are used by permission of the publisher, Tyndale House Publishers.

A portion of the poem "How the Great Guest Came" by Edwin Markham is reprinted by permission of Virgil Markham.

Abridgement of "Leisure" from *Poems of Inspiration and Courage* (1965) by Grace Noll Crowell. Copyright, 1940 by Harper & Row, Publishers, Inc.; renewed, 1968 by Grace Noll Crowell. Reprinted by permission of the publishers.

Library of Congress Cataloging in Publication Data

Boone, Charles Eugene.
　　The real Christmas.

　　　1. Christmas. I. Title.
BV45.B63   1972　　　242'.33　　　72–6299
ISBN 0–8007–0546–7

Copyright © 1961 and 1972 by Fleming H. Revell Company
All Rights Reserved
Printed in the United States of America

1708792

TO
*the choicest ornaments
around my Christmas tree
these last eighteen years—
Shirley, Cherry, Lindy, Debby and Laury.*

Contents

The Real Christmas	9
Christmas Is Always	12
Room at the Inn	17
It Can Happen to You!	24
Do You Believe in Santa Claus?	36
The Art of Giving Yourself Away	46
Follow Your Star	54
If I Could Put a Gift Under Your Tree	58

The Real Christmas

IT TAKES TWO to make Christmas. Christ—and you. Christ—and me.

That, I think, is the truth about the *real* Christmas.

This is a scientific age, my friend, and it's a scientific fact that *nothing can take place, so far as we're concerned, unless there is someone there for it to happen to or for—someone to participate or observe.* No space flight to thrill the world without an astronaut or an onlooker. No sound without a listening ear. No gift without a receiver.

Christmas, the birth of the Saviour, is the greatest event, the most joyful sound, the most perfect gift ever conceived. Wise old prophets, like Isaiah, saw it happening in the distant future:

For unto us a Child is born; unto us a Son is given; and the government shall be upon His Shoulder. These will be His royal titles: "Wonderful," "Counsellor," "The Mighty God," "The Everlasting Father," "The Prince of Peace."

His ever-expanding, peaceful government will never end. He will rule with perfect fairness and justice from the throne of his father David. He will bring true justice and peace to all the nations of the world. This is going to happen because the Lord of heaven's armies has dedicated himself to do it! (Isaiah 9:7)

And then it happened.

Jesus, the Messiah, was born almost two thousand years ago. Nobody knows whether it was really December 25 but we do know He was born. So—the most important part of the prophecy has been fulfilled. But the sad thing is that while many of us call His name Wonderful, Counsellor, The Prince of Peace, if we're honest, we have to admit that these praises ring a little hollow. His government and peace, His order and justice—far from increasing—seem a little shaky, both in our private lives and in the world around us.

Why? Because the promise wasn't kept?

Or because it hasn't become real for us yet?

Because we haven't been participators or observers? Because we haven't provided the listening ear? Or been open to receive the great gift personally?

Look back once more at the wonderful promise of Isaiah. So long *before* the great event took place in history, he claimed: "For unto us a Child is born; unto us a Son is given . . ." (Isaiah 9:6).

Now, so long *after* the birth in the manger, can we say: "For unto us . . ."?

Who was to receive the great gift?

"*Us* . . . you and me . . . and Isaiah . . . and Sam Jones next door . . . and our children . . . each individually. Each in his turn. And if enough of "us" receive it at any one time, then it will be established in the world.

But in the beginning it takes two to make the real Christmas. Christ and *us*. Christ and you. Christ and me.

When can this great event happen to us? And where? And how?

Christmas Is Always

DALE EVANS ROGERS took care of the "When?" question. She answered it simply and beautifully in *Christmas Is Always*, when she wrote:

Christmas, my child, is always.

It was always in the heart of God. It was born there. Only He could have thought of it.

Like God, Christmas is timeless and eternal, from everlasting to everlasting.

It is something even more than what happened that night in starlit little Bethlehem; it has been behind the stars forever.

Christmas is always. It has always been.

But we have not always understood it.

And, we might add, it still is today—if we understand it.

For it entered into time—our time—on that night

in Bethlehem, and the spirit of Christmas has been available to you and to me ever since. We can see evidences of it all year round in the lives of those it has touched even in a small degree. We see its light shine in strange places, and do strange things to people.

Strange, unexpected things.

I remember one Christmas Eve talking to a photographer from one of the metropolitan newspapers. Bard's regular assignment was riding the night cruiser his paper puts on the streets to follow police calls.

He and his reporter, he admitted, "specialize in chasing down catastrophe and sudden death. We're supposed to be a hard-boiled crew. But even to us, Christmas is a nightmare . . . double the drinking, shoplifting, accidents, calls for disturbing the peace . . . or at least it *was* a nightmare until one night about a week ago."

At 9:30 P.M., over their police radio came an All Units in the Vicinity call: "A missing juvenile, boy, age 11. Last seen wearing a blue flannel shirt and blue jeans."

"We were cruising in the Hollywood area where the boy was last seen," the photog said, "but who's gonna spot one eleven year old in jeans in that rush of night shoppers?"

At 10:15 P.M. he and his reporter stopped in at Hollywood police station to make a routine check, and there was Missing Juvenile in a thin flannel shirt and beat-up jeans, brought in by a burly patrolman. Under his arm he clutched a package, and he was as close to tears as a tough eleven year old could be. It was an old story, the one the desk sergeant had written down. A working mother, no father, a tough kid running loose, the mother panicky—only this one had a new twist.

"No, I won't let you see what's in my package," the boy was protesting violently. "But I'll tell you what's in it. It's a necklace and earrings." The sergeant's eyebrows shot up and his lips tightened grimly. The boy couldn't help noticing and he blurted out, "My mom saw 'em last Easter, but she couldn't afford 'em, see? I been *payin'* on 'em for eight months. Today I walked all the way to the boulevard 'cause I needed the carfare for the last payment. I was almost home when *he*"—he shot a baleful look at the patrolman—"hauls me down here. I ain't done nothin'. And if you tell my mom . . ." he was fighting those tears again— ". . . it's a Christmas surprise, see?"

The photog cleared his throat while he was telling me this part of his story. "So maybe we're a hard-boiled bunch. And suspicious. Wouldn't you be? He was a tough little kid. But I knew darn well nobody was gonna tell—*if* his story checked."

It checked. The jeweler remembered the boy well. "Been coming into my place with nickels and dimes and quarters every month since last April," he told the desk sergeant.

"Well," said the photog, "we all felt pretty good. I mean really good. Like after you've said a prayer or something. One of the prowl cars took the kid on home . . . he'd walked from way down in the south end of town . . . and the rest of us stood around that bare police station and did something I don't ever remember doing before. Even if it was only December 17 we all wished each other a Merry Christmas . . . us, newspapermen and policemen . . . the guys who thought Christmas was a nightmare! Imagine that crazy little kid—buying his mom a Christmas present, at Easter!"

But why not, if Christmas is always?

And why shouldn't it touch a bunch of "hard-boiled" men whose specialty is catastrophe and sudden death?

And why not capture a tough little kid whose beat-up shirt covered a heart that knew a lot about love?

Because love is the spirit of Christmas. Love was in the heart of God when He gave us the Gift. Love was in the heart of Christ when He lived and died for us. The Christmas spirit—love—changes hearts and lives.

When? It can happen to us now. This minute. This Christmas. In our own Hometown, U.S.A., in our own twentieth century, if we'll let Christ enter our individual minds and hearts. The minute that we do, the Child is born unto *us*. Then His government can take over our individual lives, not only on His birthday but every day. Always.

Room at the Inn

ONCE IN CALIFORNIA during the week before Christmas, Shirley, my child bride, and I were invited by some friends from Mexico to a *posada*.

Not knowing exactly what a *posada* was, we went with some curiosity and came away very much moved. The entire neighborhood in which our friends lived joined with all the guests to make it a memorable evening. It started, just as darkness fell, with a sort of procession from our hosts' hillside home—first, a lovely young girl dressed as Mary in a rough traveling cloak of blue; beside her a pious, serious older fellow as Joseph, wrapped in a homespun robe the color of earth; and behind them a serpentine of guests, including Shirl and myself, bearing lighted candles.

Up one side of the hilly street and down the other we followed the couple, and at each house where candles burned in the window (and they burned in each one) our Joseph knocked and sang a moving song in Spanish asking admittance—shelter and refuge—for the young mother-to-be by his side. In house after house Mexican singers, following the tradition of the *posada* or passage, lyrically but firmly declared that, for one reason or another, there was no room—the door closed, the hospitable candles were extinguished, and the couple moved away in the darkness to seek another door and knock again.

With repetition and the deepening night, the fact that we were in the Hollywood Hills and this was make-believe receded, and I thought I could almost feel the weariness and urgency of the need of that actual couple so many hundreds of years ago in time, and so far away in space. They had completed a long journey that night, Mary and her spouse. It had taken them maybe four or five days to cover the long miles from Nazareth to Bethlehem—over an indifferent road, through barren, desolate places, across the plains of Esdraelon, across the land of Samaria, and into Judaea, jolting along at the slow pace of Mary's donkey. And remember, this teenage girl's first baby was almost due! The city of David, Bethlehem, where Joseph must go to be taxed, was hilly too, a small town on twin hills beyond which the earth fell away again, rolling forbiddingly to the Dead Sea. But the little white town itself, Bethlehem, "the house of bread," was surrounded by fertile orchards and fields with a climate not unlike that of California.

It must have looked doubly good to the couple from Nazareth, for ". . . while they were there, the time came for her baby to be born" (Luke 2:6).

And where would her Holy Child be born?

I think we all could sense the weariness and urgency as door after door was closed until at last our *posada* returned to the house of our host and hostess, this time approaching the basement door. Again Joseph sang his plea for admittance—and this time a song of welcome greeted them, the door was thrown open wide and they stepped inside.

". . . and she gave birth to her first child, a son. She wrapped him in a blanket and laid him in a manger, because there was no room for them in the village inn" (v. 7).

It was a joyous scene that greeted Shirley and me as we too stepped through the lowly entrance—the straw and boughs of the "manger," the shepherds, the papier-maché animals, our candles making a gentle blaze of light. But for just a moment as I stood on the threshold, I couldn't help looking back over my shoulder at the dark, dark street we had left behind, and I couldn't help feeling kind of sad about those people in far-off Bethlehem *who had refused the greatest event in history;* who, for one reason or another, could not make room for the Christ Child to be born within their walls. And a sadness too, for the people today of all ages and in all places who, for one reason or another, refuse Him admittance still. In their efforts to keep their comfort and possessions, they crowd out of their lives the greatest blessings of all!

Do you believe that it still happens today? It does! And not just in certain countries or among certain groups. That very Christmas season when Shirley and I joined the *posada,* I had heard of a young couple who had been turned out of an apartment house *only four days before Christmas* by a new landlord, because their three small children made happy noises —like birds do, early in the morning. The young couple were taken in by Christian people, and I remembered very well what the young father had been quoted as saying when he brought his family to our church for help. He climaxed his story by adding wryly, "Well, here it is Christmastime again, and no room in the inn."

Yes, Christmas is always. That's the *when*. Now —and always.

But it only happens for us where love makes room. That's *where* it happens—in the minds and hearts of those who use the key of love to open the door. For our Lord Himself said: "Look! I have been standing at the door and I am constantly knocking. If anyone hears me calling him and opens the door, I will come in and fellowship with him and he with me" (Revelation 3:20).

Phillips Brooks wrote a Christmas carol once. In it he gave a clear answer to where the Christ is born today:

> Where meek souls will receive Him still,
> The dear Christ enters in.

You've never seen Him? Never heard Him knocking at your door?

Haven't you?

Remember a wonderful story told by one of America's great poets, Edwin Markham? It's about a cobbler of long ago who dearly loved the Lord. At the Christmas season he dreamed that Christ announced that He was going to pay him a personal visit the following day. So, of course, early the next morning Conrad, the cobbler, shined and decorated his meager shop, prepared a fine meal for his expected Guest, and then sat down in great expectation to await His coming. Three times that day he had visitors, but not the One he longed for.

First it was a poor beggar seeking warmth, and Conrad let him rest beside his stove and, noting that his shoes were completely worn through, gave him a stout new pair before the old man left. Then the cobbler saw an old woman, bent under a load of heavy firewood, struggling up his street, wet, weary, cold. He brought her, too, into the warmth of his humble shop—and because he had nothing else to give, he gave her part of the fine meal he had prepared for the Lord. As darkness fell, the cobbler, now impatiently waiting by his door for his overdue Visitor, saw a lost child, frightened and crying bitterly, wander into his shop. Poor Conrad was really torn, for, if he guided the child to its home, far on the other side of the city, he might miss the Christ Child. But he left the shop, hurried the child home—and hurried back.

Through what remained of the evening the cobbler worried, first that he had missed the Lord's visit, then that the Lord had decided not to make it. He imagined what bliss it would have been. Finally, he cried out: "Why is it, Lord, that your feet delay? Have you forgotten that this was the day?"

And then, in the silence, Conrad heard a soft reply:

> Lift up your heart for I kept my word.
> Three times I came to your friendly door;
> Three times my shadow was on your floor.
> I was the beggar with bruised feet;
> I was the woman you gave to eat:
> I was the child on the homeless street.

You see? The humble cobbler's shop had become an inn where there was room. So had the home of our church members who welcomed the homeless young family and their three children.

In each case, a place had been prepared for Him . . . love had opened the door . . . and He came.

It Can Happen to You!

How is a place to be prepared for Him, the Christ Child?

The actual Incarnation in time, in history, took place through Mary, a teenager. (Or didn't you know that Mary is believed to have been so young?) And Mary has been called a key for humanity.

Yet there are only two events in Mary's life—before the great night in Bethlehem—that the writers of the gospels considered significant enough to record. You know, I think there are clues here for those of us who today would like to make Christmas real in our own lives.

First, when the angel of God appeared to her and summoned her to her great task, Mary surrendered. There was no hesitation—no "What will I have to sacrifice?" When her moment of decision came she asked one shy question, and then replied with her whole heart: "I am the Lord's servant, and I am willing to do whatever he wants" (Luke 1:38).

In his book, *Jesus and His Times*, Daniel-Rops comments: "She accepted her destiny, putting herself body and soul, her honor and her worldly prospects, into the hands of God."

Now, this describes surrender at the level of purity and beauty and trust that Mary had already achieved. But I think you and I can make a beginning at whatever level we find ourselves—if we say, and sincerely mean, the lines of surrender proposed by our Lord in His prayer: "Thy will be done!"

That then would be our first step of preparation, an act of surrender of our will and lives to God. This is a quiet step, taken somewhere deep inside.

But immediately, Mary took another one. An outward step. This young girl hurried into the rugged hill country to visit her cousin, Elizabeth. The angel Gabriel had told her that Elizabeth was six months with child, although this cousin was "in her old age" and had been called "barren."

It seems Mary went on her journey not only to confirm the miracle that had been announced by Gabriel—she could have done that at a glance, or in a day or two—but *to be of service* to her elderly cousin in her time of need, for Mary stayed with Elizabeth three months, long enough for a child to be born to the "old" and formerly "barren" woman.

In other words, having been overshadowed by the Spirit of God, Mary felt impelled to go immediately and offer her help to someone in need. And she went. I guess the question I must ask myself is whether or not I'd do the same. Considering Mary's behavior, I would think the true handmaid or servant of God must be willing to go into action for Him as a part of accepting His will.

It was only after both her *inward surrender* and her *outward action* that the wonderful words burst from Mary, "Oh, how I praise the Lord. How I rejoice in God my Savior!" (Luke 1:46, 47).

Now. Can you and I, in so many ways imperfect, in so many ways impure, hope to find the right road to the Child's birthplace? Can it happen to us today? How do we accomplish it? Well—let's ponder a little more.

In Bethlehem itself I find two more significant events recorded that seem to offer further clues on how we get ready for His birth in our lives. The one is told in the Gospel of Luke, the other in the Gospel of Matthew. And it seems to me that each represents a different type of preparation . . . for a different type of person. One is the approach of the heart. The other—of the mind.

Luke, a Greek physician, a very learned man, strangely enough is the one who describes the approach of the heart. Tradition says that he may have talked to Mary, and perhaps it was from her that he got this beautiful report—for it's at the conclusion of it that he announces, ". . . but Mary quietly treasured these things in her heart and often thought about them" (Luke 2:19).

There were, says Luke, shepherds watching over their flocks in the hills and caves around Bethlehem that marvelous night. And an angel of the Lord appeared to them, and the glory of the Lord shone around them, and the angel said:

> "Don't be afraid! I bring you the most joyful news ever announced, and it is for everyone! The Savior—yes, the Messiah, the Lord—has been born tonight in Bethlehem! How will you recognize him? You will find a baby wrapped in a blanket, lying in a manger!" Suddenly, the angel was joined by a vast host of others—the armies of heaven—praising God: "Glory to God in the highest heaven," they sang, "and peace on earth for all those pleasing him." They ran to the village and found their way to Mary and Joseph. And there was the baby, lying in the manger (Luke 2:10–14, 16).

The first, then, to recognize that the old prophecies had been fulfilled, to participate in the great event, to hear the glad sounds that "it is for everyone," to rush to receive the gift—were simply humble country shepherds. They were probably poor, certainly "underprivileged," most likely uneducated. They had nothing to bring to the wondrous Child but *themselves*—their awe, and belief, and love. But our learned friend Luke makes it very clear that it was exactly these simple folk who were the *first* to celebrate Christmas, and to carry the news to all people.

Today many would scoff at the idea that an angel might in this age appear to man to guide him to the manger. But wait—who are *we* to limit what the God of love will do? Christians know better.

I'm thinking this minute of the heartwarming story of Kathy Morrison, a fifteen-year-old girl who was picked up as a vagrant in a big Midwestern city and taken to Juvenile Hall. She had no baggage, no coat, no destination, but she did have a brassy manner, bleached hair, clouded eyes, chipped finger nails, and an incredible tale to tell.

For the past year, off and on, she had been the human target for a knife-throwing act in a traveling carnival! Her most productive schooling was a trick taught her by the carnival manager whereby she could slip the customer change for a dollar when he had given her a ten. Her chief accomplishment was her ability to dodge knives when one of the members of the act had been drinking.

The juvenile court judge found that Kathy came originally from a farming community. Her father had died when she was eleven and when her mother remarried, the girl was only an unwanted mouth to feed around the ramshackle home of her stepfather. It was a cheerless, godless household, plagued with liquor, obscene language and physical violence. Kathy was forced to quit school and hire out as a chore girl *to pay board and room to her stepfather*. At fourteen!

No one bothered to look for her, and after a series of unhappy experiences as a farm maid, she met up with the carnival. After joining them, she made ten to fifteen dollars a night at her hazardous work, both in front of the knife-throwers, thrilling the customers, and behind the little cashier's coop, shortchanging them. But the money just "ran away" . . . on "picture shows," hair bleach, clothes, gadgets, and sweets . . . until, when the carnival broke up, she found herself out of a job, out of money, and in Juvenile Hall.

The judge asked her if she had any relatives, any

place she'd like to go. No—no relatives, she told him, but there was a *place* . . . once when the knife-throwers were going on a "binge" they checked her at the Sunshine Mission just off the city's skid row. "I spent Christmas there," she told the judge wistfully. "The lady let me help her . . . she was a nice lady . . . smiled a lot, y'know. . . . She let me be an angel in the pageant. I liked being an angel . . . I liked the story about the Little Baby. . . ."

And so, on the judge's recommendation, Kathy went back to the "wonderful lady" at the Sunshine Mission as a dishwasher and general chore girl. She didn't know she was "underprivileged" as she helped the missionary tend her flock by night and day. I know, because I've heard from her several times since then.

Kathy Morrison has a new name now—and she's very grown-up. She knows that the Little Baby is the Christ Child and she gives Him her awe and her belief and her love. She wouldn't trade places with anyone in the world, because today—as part of the permanent mission staff and the "wonderful lady's" first assistant—she can play the Christmas angel three hundred and sixty-five days a year.

And that's the first way—the way of the shepherds.

The way of Kathy Morrison.

It's the simplest way.

It's the quickest way.

It's the way of the open heart and unquestioning faith.

But somehow it isn't possible to all of us—at least at first. And so *there's another way*—the one described by Matthew—the way of the mind. Matthew tells us that there also came to Bethlehem to participate in the great event "some [astronomers] from eastern lands." And they weren't looking for a baby. They wanted a figure of power. "Where," they wanted to know, "is the newborn King of the Jews? for we have seen his star in far-off eastern lands, and have come to worship him" (Matthew 2:2).

These astronomers—or students of the stars, from the East—are sometimes referred to as the Magi The word *Magi* originally denoted a priestly caste of the Medes and Persians—but had come to mean Oriental sages or philosophers, experts in things intellectual as well as spiritual.

They were men whose minds were full of questions. We'd naturally suppose that they were older, had traveled farther, were men of more substance, and certainly of more complicated personalities when they found their way to the Christ Child than were the shepherds. But they *did* find the way, and when they arrived they brought symbolic gifts: gold for a king, frankincense for a God, myrrh for the bitterness of the Man foreordained to death.

For a lot of us this longer road, the one of mingled faith and doubt, of trials and errors, of questioning and superstitions, is the only one open. It's a long mental and physical journey—but with determination and a desire to worship the true King, we *can* arrive.

Will this way really work in a skeptical and scientific age?

Here's an example of how pondering the story of the Magi enriched one man's life . . . and touched the lives of millions more.

His mother read the story of the Wise Men to Lew Wallace when he was a small boy, long before the turn of the twentieth century. And it filled the small boy with a continuing wonder. Who were they? From where did they come? Exactly what brought them to Jerusalem that certain night with their great question, "Where is the newborn King of the Jews?" (Matthew 2:2).

The little boy grew into a young man and, as he continued to ponder these questions, his imagination led him to write down a story which started with the

Wise Men in the East and ended in Bethlehem, but he hadn't the courage to send it to a publisher.

Time passed and Lew Wallace became busy about many things. His interest in the story dwindled and his attitude toward religion became, according to him, "one of absolute indifference. I had heard it argued times innumerable, always without interest."

From his own description he would appear to have much in common with some folks today—too lazy even to be an active agnostic, he seems to have become what I call a "shoulder shrugger." And then, on a train bound for Indianapolis, Lew Wallace had a session with Colonel Robert G. Ingersoll, one of the best-known and most active agnostics of his day.

Wallace describes how Colonel Ingersoll held him "spellbound, listening to a medley of arguments, eloquence, wit, satire, audacity, irreverence, poetry, brilliant antithesis, and pungent excoriation of believers in God, Christ, and heaven, the like of which I had never heard."

Most of us in this day and age have heard a similar medley. It is played all round us, like the records on the juke box. And if it does to us what it did to Lew Wallace, then there's every chance that we, too, may become wise men—as he did.

[For it served to] lift me out of my indifference . . . I [was] now moved as never before, and by what? The most outright denials of all human knowledge of God, Christ, and the hereafter which figures so in the hope and faith of the believing everywhere . . . I was ashamed of my ignorance . . . I was aroused for the first time in my life to the importance of religion.

. . . I resolved to study the subject. And while casting round how to set about the study to the best advantage, I thought of the manuscript in my desk. Its closing scene was the Child Christ in the cave by Bethlehem. Why not go on with the story down to the Crucifixion? That would make a book, and compel me to study everything of pertinency; after which, possibly, I would be possessed of opinions of real value.

And he brought his gift to the Christ Child, too—for he concludes:

It only remains to say that I did as resolved, with results—first the book *Ben-Hur*, and second, a conviction amounting to absolute belief in God and the divinity of Christ.

It's a good story for us to remember in this day when materialistic psychology and godless political philosophies are making the discordant music of the Antichrist all around us. You could sum it up in the words of another wise man, Sir Francis Bacon, who wrote in the seventeenth century: "A little philosophy inclineth man's mind to atheism, but depth in philosophy bringeth men's minds about to religion."

This is the way of the Wise Men—the way of the intellect.

It's the harder way.
It's the longer way.

But both roads, the simple one the country shepherds traveled, and the distant roads of the Magi, led them to the first Christmas. And, my friend, if you and I will follow either one, it can happen to us!

Do You Believe in Santa Claus?

THE THINGS WE'VE been talking about are, I guess, what you'd call the *deep things* of Christmas—the very solemn, very holy things.

To me they come first because they are the *real* Christmas, the *always* Christmas, but that doesn't mean that there isn't a very special place in our lives for the Christmas holiday and all the special symbols and reminders and festivities we look forward to each year. The story, as I see it, has grown and grown, taking in all loving hearts and customs until it includes sleigh bells, and mistletoe, and gaily-colored packages, and Santa Claus—and even Rudolph!

Personally, I like that little Rudolph fella—the most modern addition to the Christmas scene. Rudolph has added a twentieth-century lilt to all those other traditions that have been handed down from generation to generation. Rudolph is *our* contribution—a sort of teenager in the ranks of venerable manger animals.

Speaking of teenagers, there's one aspect of Christmas that belongs exclusively to them. The idea came to me when Shirl and I were wrapping packages to put under our tree and I was reminiscing about the ol' school days.

Anyway, I told Shirley about a time when I was in the tenth grade and we were asked to write an English composition on the quotation: "The child is father to the man." One girl wrote, "This is a curious saying which has more in it than you would think. It doesn't sound possible, but then poets often say impossible things so long as they rhyme."

And, said I, "I've just made up a curious saying for Christmas. It also has more in it than you may think. Try this on for size: 'The Teenager of Today is Father to the Santa Claus of Tomorrow.'" The good wife shook her head in bewilderment at her poor demented hubby. Now, I'll admit that we singers also have been known to sing impossible things so long as they rhyme, but this doesn't happen to be one of 'em.

It's a simple little thought, really—and I share it with you teenagers because, while you never come right out and ask if *I* believe in Santa Claus, you've told me quite frankly that *you* don't, and assumed that at my more advanced age of course I don't either.

But hold on there, pardner—I *do!*

I not only believe, I *know* that there's a Santa Claus; and to me it seems very important that you should know it, too, because what kind of a fellow he's going to be in five or ten years' time depends on that.

Now, I don't deny going through the stage of unbelief myself. I remember only too well the year that I, who was fascinated by everything about St. Nick, from the smallest curl in his white beard to the tip of Rudolph's red nose, discovered behind the masquerade none other than those beloved but familiar forms, my beardless dad and reindeerless mama. Right then—as suddenly as a candle dies in a hurricane—a certain magic quality went out of my holidays. How could I ever really look forward to Christmas again?

The teenage years ran out for me before that particular magic was rekindled, before the Christmas rolled around when I found Santa Claus again, not as a fairy-tale friend from the North Pole, but as a reality. I was a grown man then, the head of a household, an adult of twenty-one with a ravishingly beautiful wife and a baby daughter—and it was little Cherry who brought back the magic.

One year when Shirley and I were rummaging through some Christmas boxes to decorate our house for our *four* daughters, an eighteen-year-old neighbor came in to help us. Margaret's mother had been dead for many years and she said rather wistfully, "I think the greatest thing in the world at Christmas must be to have a mother."

Shirley looked at her a moment and then shook her head. "The greatest thing in the world is to *be* a mother," she said.

And I couldn't help thinking that since that night when Shirley and I filled that first tiny stocking for that first small Boonelet I had known that the great thing is not to *believe* in Santa Claus. It is to *be* Santa Claus. And now, three daughters later, I was three times as sure. But between the year that the magic died and the year it was rekindled ran a long ribbon of time. I had to learn a lot of things, things that perhaps, if I can pass 'em along to you, will help you get more out of Christmas this year and rediscover Santa Claus right now.

Do you know how important I think this is? Can you believe that I'm not just indulging a holiday fantasy? Look, I know some of the soul-searching you're going through, especially you teenagers. I know you're asking the same questions I asked—big, important questions: "What is life all about?"—"Is there a purpose to it?"—"What can I do that's important, really worth anything?" I know too, this Santa Claus business naturally gets shoved way into the background while you try to work out these big "whats." But oddly, in pondering the real meaning of Christmas, I begin to glimpse some of the very answers you're wanting.

We've already talked about some of them—but now I want you to understand why old St. Nicholas once again became important to me, and the magic of believing became important too—as it will to you.

For day after tomorrow, or the year after next, you will find, as Shirley and I did, that as each generation graduates into the adult realm, it becomes the custodian of Christmas, keepers of its traditions and customs, of its beauty and inspiration, a link in a chain which has been forged generation by generation for almost two thousand years. Tomorrow it will be in your hands to keep Christmas, and it will mean to your children what you make it mean—*and that can only be whatever it means to you.*

In the Bible you'll read Paul's words: "It's like this: when I was a child I spoke and thought and reasoned as a child does. But when I became a man my thoughts grew far beyond those of my childhood, and now I have put away the childish things" (1 Corinthians 13:11).

Now, for sure the teen age is the "putting away" time and it isn't as grim or stern as it sounds. Instead it's very exciting, an adventure, a voyage of discovery. In the case of Christmas, we shouldn't lose the trimming and the gaiety—instead it's a matter of *putting away our belief in the symbols themselves and finding out what the symbols stand for*—what is truly behind Santa's beard, and under the mistletoe, and at the heart of the gaily-wrapped packages, and shining from the star on top of our tree. And then, you see, the symbol becomes even more wonderful as a significant part of keeping the real Christmas, and the magic burns brighter as we realize that each year we are hosts and hostesses at His birthday party.

Just who is this jolly gent we call Santa Claus?

Well, to begin historically, and even myths have their history, the wonderful ruddy fellow in red velvet with his white fur, his tasseled cap and his remarkable generosity, is of mixed nationality. He's part Lycian, part Italian, part Dutch, part English. In character he's probably three parts the Dutch St.

Nicholas and one part the British Father Christmas. All these were blended in the mighty melting pot of the United States to give him birth as we know him today.

The original St. Nicholas known in medieval legends is really a combination of two bishops, both from what today is called Turkey. One of them, Nicholas of Myra, is believed to have died in the fourth century. The other, Nicholas of Pinora, died in 564. Both actually lived, but further than that we know nothing except that they merged into a kind of saintly miracle worker.

Early in the eleventh century, when Myra was overrun by the Mohammedans, some merchants lovingly transported their saint's bones to a seaport in Southern Italy and from there sailors carried stories of St. Nicholas to all of western and northern Europe, recommending him as kind of a patron saint of seafaring men. By the thirteenth century, Holland had no less than twenty-three St. Nicholas churches, and by the fourteenth century choir boys of these churches were being given some money and a holiday on the date in December assigned to St. Nicholas. A little later, on the same day, the schools of Holland began to reward diligent, "good" pupils with a gift while lazy or naughty pupils were punished with a birch switch (how do you think the kids would like that arrangement today?), both functions performed by a teacher dressed in a red mantle and wearing a white beard to represent the good bishop. Gradually, the idea spread to include all children in the gift giving and grew into a wonderful celebration.

Now, how did Santa get to America? Well, when the early Dutch settlers came to America they couldn't leave their good bishop behind and so Sinterklaas, as they called him, landed on our shores. Later he was joined by the jolly round figure in high boots imported by the British, their beloved Father Christmas. Since both had celebrations in December and, since their ideas were so compatible, they merged into one figure, keeping the Dutch name, Sinterklaas, and thus was Santa Claus born.

This is the history of a myth, but out of the myth has come a spirit that has helped many to understand the real Christmas—the true story of the greatest Gift ever given. And whenever that spirit prompts you to give something of yourself to someone else, in love, unselfishly—then the real Santa Claus is in action again.

If Santa has become commercial, it's not because either St. Nicholas or Father Christmas took Christ out of Christmas. No, we can't blame anybody but ourselves for that, and since it's you and I who re-enact the ancient role, it's up to us to make Jesus the central figure. Surely Santa as he *should* be, as little children see him, a symbol of love, of generosity, of merriment, would have delighted the heart of the Christ Child.

And along with Santa in our country come other customs from other lands, which make more festive His birthday. One is the Christmas tree, another the mistletoe.

Mistletoe crept into the feast of Christmas as part of the ritual celebrated at the court of King Arthur and his Knights of the Round Table. They called it "all-heal" and believed that all who wore a sprig about their neck were insuring their health and protecting themselves from physical evil. (What with germs and virus bugs, the way we use mistletoe today would more likely produce the opposite results, wouldn't it?)

The custom of kissing one "caught" under the mistletoe had a significance that, if we were to adopt it, would certainly be a great birthday gift for the Prince of Peace. Centuries ago in England, if two warriors happened to meet under a tree to which mistletoe had attached itself, they immediately dropped their weapons and embraced!

I can think of several "summits" where a bough draped with mistletoe might have come in handy. If the men from opposing governments meeting under it had honored the old tradition, it might have helped fulfill the promise of Isaiah for His Kingdom! I'm referring to the one about establishing His Kingdom and peace in the world.

Now, the Christmas tree was part of the winter solstice feast called Yule, celebrated in Germany as well as England. Since in pagan days this was a celebration of the return of the sun after winter's dark, the trees were hung with blossoms to welcome the coming Spring. (I've seen 'em do that in Hollywood when they're making a Spring movie in the Fall.) In Scandinavia this custom was adapted to the spirit of Christmas giving, and the trees were hung with bits of bread and cake for the hungry birds on the birthday of the Infant Jesus. Flowers and food, then, were the first ornaments to adorn the tree around which old Saint Nick would place his gifts.

But back to the question, "Who *is* Santa Claus?" Here is the real magic. Here is an answer to that other question: "What can I do that's important, worthwhile?" For Santa Claus, as you've guessed, is none other than *you and me!* It's any individual, on Christmas day and every other day, who is willing to let the true spirit of giving into his or her heart.

Remember? It takes two to make Christmas. Christ and you. Christ and me.

The Art of Giving Yourself Away

YOU KNOW, WE'RE born with the spirit of *getting* (at least I was!) and we develop the spirit of *giving* only after we recognize the childish "gimmes" and are willing to grow out of them.

I remember a wonderful story Robert Young told about his youngest daughter and the night she began to grow up for sure—to "put away the childish things." Until then, according to Bob, the evening prayers she said while they knelt beside her bed sounded more like a kid's letter to Santa Claus than anything else. "She'd reel off a list of things she wanted done and while they changed from time to time, the list didn't seem to get shorter. Then one night when she had plowed confidently through her requests there was quite a pause without the final 'amen.' I just knelt there and waited and finally she said, in a very small voice, as if she had heard what she was saying for the first time: 'And now, dear Lord, is there anything I can do for you?' "

And that seems to me to be the place where I always have to start my Christmas giving. After all, I remind myself, whose birthday is it, anyway? I knew a little boy whose mother told him Christmas was Jesus' birthday and immediately he demanded: "How many candles does *He* have on *His* cake?" Now I somehow don't think with all those stars of His He needs any candles on a cake—but there *are* things we can do for Him, things He asked us to do in connection with *giving*. He mentioned a *step of preparation for giving* which should come first: "So if you are standing before the altar in the Temple, offering a sacrifice to God, and suddenly remember that a friend has something against you, leave your sacrifice there beside the altar and go and apologize and be reconciled to him, and then come and offer your sacrifice to God" (Matthew 5:23, 24).

Now, that's plain enough even for me to understand—and what a wonderful spirit in which to approach Christmas! Wouldn't that be a great gift for the One whose message was "Love each other . . ." (John 13:34) if, before Christmas day, each one of us who professes to follow Him actually went around and called on each individual who is mad at us or whom we have hurt, each one with whom we've had a hassle or who has hurt us, so that we didn't have a bad friend, or a hurt feeling, or a hate, or resentment, in our whole beings? Imagine if everyone who celebrated Christmas did this! I've got a feeling it would be a hundred times as sensational and a thousand times more useful to mankind than landing something or someone on the moon!

But the only place we can begin is with ourselves —and maybe by suggesting it to a couple of close friends as an experiment. I mean, really do it, too— not just think about it! Then, having made our preparation for giving as He asked us to, what more could we do for Him? Well, let's see.

We're told: "The star appeared again, standing over Bethlehem. Their joy knew no bounds!" (Matthew 2:9, 10). This rejoicing wasn't meant for only the Wise Men—the privilege wasn't reserved for just a few—so any time we sing Christmas carols and really put our hearts into them, really *know* what we're saying and whom we're praising and where our joy is coming from—we're expressing our gladness and spreading it around a little bit. Of course, I'm partial to singing anyway, but we're told the skies were filled with heavenly music, and I'll bet the

Child would love to hear all kinds of people serenading Him at His birthday party. And the psalmist David says: "Go through his open gates with great thanksgiving; enter his courts with praise" (Psalms 100:4).

"Be of good cheer," Jesus said on several occasions, and certainly the birth of Christ into the world is an occasion of joy. The poet Carpini once asked his friend, the great composer Haydn, how it happened that his church music was always of an animated, cheerful character. Haydn replied: "I cannot make it otherwise. I write according to the thoughts which I feel. When I think upon God, my heart is so full of joy that the notes dance and leap, as it were, from my pen; and since God has given me a cheerful heart, it will be easily forgiven me that I serve Him with a cheerful spirit."

And so you too, my friend, can give to Him the gift of a cheerful spirit, a sign of joy and trust in His presence—the gift of praise to our most worthy King.

And what about giving to others? Well, this is very important on His birthday. Didn't He, Himself, say: "When you did it to these my brothers you were doing it to me" (Matthew 25:40)? But He did *not* say we had to run out and blow next year's allowance buying expensive gifts. Quite the contrary: "And if, as my representatives, you give even a cup of cold water to a little child . . ." (Matthew 10:42). Remember Conrad, the cobbler?

There are things you can *do* that will be appreciated more than the things money can buy. Believe me! It's a kind of challenge to see how many ways you can find to "give yourself away." If you know a mother who would like to go out to church, or some other activity, who can't afford a baby-sitter . . . well, you take it from there. If you're a boy with a car . . . need I say more?

For a few pennies (the last time I looked) you can send cards or notes to people who would least expect to hear from you (check that relative list carefully!); the people we encounter but don't really know, the driver of your school bus, the officer who directs traffic at your corner, shut-ins of your own age in hospitals, best of all, to anyone you've ever been mad at.

It's possible sometimes to make visits to hospitals, orphanages, or to help a family in trouble. I know one mother, daughter and son who do their "spring cleaning" just before Christmas and, although they're folks without much money, they always have such a big box to give away that they say, "It makes us feel quite rich!"

One school group in Bergen County, New Jersey, actually combed their town to find "the least of their brethren," then began to collect a Christmas fund in a big empty jar. On Christmas Day there was enough in the jar for Christmas dinners and gifts for two families. Had they deprived themselves a little to do this? Might be good if they did—don't you think so?

Don't ever be afraid that this kind of giving will impoverish you. This isn't the kind of giving that runs people into debt. Instead it builds up a backlog of security feelings. You begin to be able to answer those big questions. "What is life all about?"—"Does it have a meaning and a purpose?"—"What am I supposed to do here?" And the answer is that we are to *contribute* to life, to enrich the lives of others, to give all the love we have, all the time we have, all the thoughtfulness and kindness we have to making the world a happier place because we were born into it. It's our duty . . . *and* our privilege. As a very wise woman once said:

Christ has no body now on earth but *yours,*
No hands but *yours,* no feet but *yours;*

Yours are the eyes through which Christ's compassion is to look out on the world;

Yours are the feet with which He is to go about doing good,

And *yours* are the hands with which He is to bless us *now*.

Does this sound like a tall order? It is. Do I do it all the time? I don't. I only try, and not as much as I should. That's all that's asked of you, though. Just try, and don't be self-conscious or afraid you've nothing to give. Everyone has. And the rewards are great. There was a little box in *Guideposts* magazine one December that turned me on.

WHAT DOES THE BIBLE SAY ABOUT GIVING?

The Lord's request	Malachi 3:10
Who shall give?	Deuteronomy 16:17
How much?	Genesis 28:22
In what spirit?	II Corinthians 9:7
When to give	I Corinthians 16:2

I always like to remember the story of the country minister who had no regular congregation and earned his living filling vacancies around the countryside. One Sunday he was called to preach in a small-town church and as he went in he and his little boy passed a box labeled: FOR THE POOR. Although he wasn't overburdened with wealth himself, he fished out a quarter and dropped it in. At the end of the service he was informed that visiting ministers were paid with the contents of the Poor Box. When it was opened, out rolled one lone quarter—his own. "Gee, Dad," said his son, "you'd have gotten more out if you'd put more in."

Christmas is a good time to take stock of our balance with the world. Let's face it—God has been pretty good to us, hasn't He? Are we giving Him anything in return?

Follow Your Star

ON TOP OF OUR CHRISTMAS trees, hanging over our streets, adorning our Christmas packages each year is the bright star of Bethlehem.

Did you ever stop to wonder whether, if you had lived in Bethlehem all those years ago, you would have been one of those to follow that star, to see the manger and the Infant? I don't think I would have —for we remember it was only the Magi, the Wise Men from the East, who saw the star—and the shepherds, the humble ones, who heard angel voices, who followed to worship and lay their gifts at His feet. Nobody else knew what it meant then.

I'm afraid I wouldn't qualify. I've never been a Wise Man, and nobody ever accused me of being overly humble. I've had absolutely no experience as a shepherd! But I pray a lot these days—for wisdom *and* humility. *I need a star to follow* and guidance from above if I'm going to find my way!

I can see every year, in store windows, in churches, in homes, in pictures, plays, and processions, the concept various people have of the scene that greeted those fortunate ones who followed the star. This perhaps is one of the most universal ways of keeping Christmas a fresh, new, vital experience. It began back in 1223 when Francis of Assisi wished to dramatize the story of the Christ Child with real people, real animals, a real manger, in such a way that rich and poor, young and old, could grasp the significance of this First Birthday. Today in Italy the mountain cave where it was held is called the *Presepio*, the crib. In France, such scenes have become the *Crèche*. In Mexico the *Nacimiento*. In our own country it's the *Nativity*.

Now the Nativity includes not only the Child, but the holy family—and this can carry us one step farther in keeping Christmas fresh and green. You see, His birthday can be a family day, a day to reestablish *our* family unity—when we *give* with love, and *receive* with honest appreciation. We might even get around to appreciating some of the things that we've received throughout the year through our family, that may have gone unnoticed.

Shirley and I are family as well as church folks. We work at it. We work at it over the Christmas season—but not in a breathless, rush-rush, shop-til-the-last-minute way. Not if we can help it, anyway. I remember a poem I read that slowed me down considerably in the old, hectic holiday preparation department. It's another item for pondering called, "Leisure," written by Grace Noll Crowell:

> I shall attend to my little errands of love
> Early, this year,
> That the brief days before Christmas may be
> Unhampered and clear
> Of the fever of hurry. The breathless rushing that I
> Have known in the past
> Shall not possess me; I shall be calm in my soul
> And ready at last
> For Christmas. . . .
> . . . .
> I shall have leisure—I shall go out alone
> From my roof and my door;
> I shall not miss the silver silence of stars
> As I have before,
> And oh, perhaps, if I stand there very still,
> And very long,
> I shall hear what the clamor of living has kept from me:
> The angels' song!

To enjoy Christmas as a family we make our preparations early, decorate the house, buy and sometimes make and wrap our gifts so that when Christmas Eve rolls around and then *the* day—we can *enjoy* it!—in our church, in our home, with our children, our families, with each other.

Honestly, the very best things we have found are right there.

If I Could Put a Gift Under Your Tree

I'D MAKE SURE each and every one of you had a Bible of your own, if you don't have one already. (And if I were picking it out, I'd give you a *New American Standard* or a *Living Bible*.) It tells the whole Christmas story so much better than I can and you could read it any day of the year. And for me, the answers to all my Big Questions I have found on its pages. Abraham Lincoln once said to a delegation which gave him a Bible: "This great Book . . . is the best gift God has given man. . . . But for it we could not know right from wrong."

Actually, I'd disagree with Uncle Abe about which is the best gift; God tells us Himself that His Son Jesus is the *best* expression of His love toward man (John 3:16). But the Bible *is* the written account of that priceless Gift.

And with the Bible I'd leave a bookmark from my scrapbook—and since you probably already have your Bible (and, if not, maybe you asked Santa for one this year), I'll give you the bookmark anyhow:

Remedies for Trouble

If you are down with the blues, read the Twenty-Third Psalm.

If there is a chilly sensation about the heart, read the third chapter of Revelation.

If you don't know where to look to meet family fund difficulties, read the Twenty-Seventh Psalm.

If you are lonesome and unprotected, read the Ninety-First Psalm.

If the plumbing is leaking, wrap up the pipe and wash your hands and read the first chapter of St. James.

If you find yourself losing confidence in men read the thirteenth chapter of I Corinthians.

If people pelt you with hard words, read the fifteenth chapter of St. John and the Fifty-First Psalm.

If you are out of sorts, read the twelfth chapter of Hebrews.

On the card, under the Bethlehem star, I'd write, in the words of that great little guy, Tiny Tim, "God bless us every one!" Or in the beautiful words of a man who lived in the sixteenth century:

I am your friend, and my love for you goes deep.
> There is nothing I can give you which you have not got;
But there is much, very much, that, while I cannot give it,
> You can take.

No heaven can come to us unless our hearts
> Find rest in today. Take Heaven!
No peace lies in the future which is not hidden
> In this present little instant. Take Peace!

The gloom of the world is but a shadow.
> Behind it, yet within our reach, is Joy.
There is radiance and glory in the darkness,
> Could we but see, and to see, we have only to look.
I beseech you to look.

Life is so generous a giver, but we,
> Judging its gifts by their covering,
Cast them away as ugly, or heavy, or hard.
> Remove the covering, and you will find beneath it
A living splendor, woven of love, by wisdom, with power.

Welcome it, grasp it, and you touch the
> Angel's hand that brings it to you.
Everything we call a trial, a sorrow, or a duty,
> Believe me, that Angel's hand is there; the gift is there,

And the wonder of an overshadowing Presence.

Our joys too: be not content with them as joys.
They, too, conceal diviner gifts.

Life is so full of meaning and purpose,
So full of Beauty—beneath its covering—
That you will find earth but cloaks your heaven.
Courage then to claim it: that is all!
But courage you have; and the knowledge that we
Are pilgrims together,
Wending through unknown country, home.

And so, at this time, I greet you.
Not quite as the world sends greetings.
But with profound esteem and with the prayer
That for you now and forever,
The day breaks, and the shadows flee away.

And then I'd sign the card, "Merry Christmas!"

These things I'd put under your tree, but my resources are very limited. What would God like to give you this Christmas?

My friend—your Heavenly Father wants to give you the most precious gifts in all creation! Love, joy, peace—and Himself—personally delivered by His own Holy Spirit!

In Romans 5:5, He tells us that ". . . we feel this warm love everywhere within us because God has given us the Holy Spirit to fill our hearts with his love."

In Galatians 5:22, He shows us that ". . . when the Holy Spirit controls our lives he will produce this kind of fruit in us: love, joy, peace . . . ."

Simon Peter, announcing to thousands of assembled Jews in Acts 2 said: "Each one of you must turn from sin, return to God, and be baptized in the name of Jesus Christ for the forgiveness of your sins; then you also shall receive this gift, the Holy Spirit. For Christ promised him to each one of you who has been called by the Lord our God . . ." (vs. 38, 39).

Do you understand? God wants to give you, personally, His own Presence, His own attributes, His own Holy Spirit!

Jesus, whose birthday is Christmas, says in John 14 that He will give His friends the Comforter—the Holy Spirit—to instruct, encourage and guide them. He said, "he . . . shall be in you" (v. 17).

Hear Him, the Prince of Peace: "I am leaving you with a gift—peace of mind and heart! And the peace I give isn't fragile like the peace the world gives . . ." (v. 27).

No, Jesus doesn't send this gift airmail or parcel post. Listen: " . . . I will only reveal myself to those who love and obey me. The Father will love them too, and we will come to them and live with them" (v. 23).

We will come to them!

"I have been standing at the door and I am constantly knocking," He said in Revelation 3:20. "If anyone hears me calling him and opens the door, I will come in and fellowship with him and he with me."

Dear friend, lay my meager gifts aside for awhile. Hear His voice, open the door of your heart, receive the gift of His Holy Spirit—and enjoy the glory of Jesus at your own tree, and the joy of that personal Star.

Allow Him to be—in the union of your spirits—your real Christmas.

Didn't I say, in the beginning, it takes two?

Christ and you?

Hallelujah!